The Srampagmano Tales

by

Scarlett Parker

with illustrations by

Faith Buck

ISBN 978 1 291 12782 9

For Tynan.
I'll see you up the road . . .

Contents

Prologue 7

The Roadie's Tale.................... 15

The Courier's Tale.................... 21

The Sportiviste's Tale 25

The Trackie's Tale.................... 29

The Rouleur's Tale 33

The Fakenger's Tale 37

The Randonneur's Tale.................... 41

The Tester's Tale 45

The Grimpeur's Tale.................... 49

Epilogue.................... 53

Prologue

If riding every day would get you wet
A dozen times the annual estimate
It's no surprise that after April showers
When country lanes are lined with wild flowers
The winter gravel washed towards the verges
And framing tarmacadam which emerges
A restlessness in London starts to heighten
As cyclists decide to ride to Brighton
Dissociated from the daily grind
They swiftly leave the city far behind
Rejoicing in their union with the vélo
But disinclined to wear fluorescent yellow
With strong resolve their legs refuse to weaken
At least until they've crested Ditchling Beacon
They'll finally come to rest down by the pier
Then feast on fish and chips and pints of beer.

And so by chance one morning in mid-May
While finishing my first cup of the day
Espresso, double, from Look Mum No Hands
A rendezvous for London's cycling fans
The final preparations for my ride
A pilgrimage of sorts to the seaside
Were interrupted when out of the blue
Some other riders stopped to grab a brew

With keen eyes trained on all the bikes outside
They shuffled in to stock up for their ride
I quietly noted those who shuffled best
Were those, like me, whose cleats were well recessed
The ambience promoted interaction
Revealing things in common with their faction
We'd all made plans to cycle to the coast
Which prompted a suggestion from our host:
"Amongst a group as disparate as yours
Combining your accumulated tours
Would surely conjure stories to be told
Which like the roads in front of you unfold
For roads and stories each have their beginning
The middle's navigated via spinning
And once you've finally made it to the end
What better than to share it with a friend?"
Our embryonic peloton concurred
We'd supplement our journey with the word
The union of inches, gear and column
To save our voyage from becoming solemn
A paragraph accompanying each mile
The rhythm unrelenting, pulsatile
And best of all, annoying clicks and creaks
Would not be noticed while each rider speaks.

Before the riders' journey has begun
I'll introduce you to them one by one
A brief description capturing their essence
The tribe for which they represent quintessence.

There is a roadie, cycling's shining knight
A lycra suit of armour, sleek and tight
Whatever discipline you care to mention
He's no doubt at some point been in contention
Encapsulating every rider type
Perpetuating mystery and hype
His pins are chiselled, shaven, lean, and tanned
Performing feats that most can't understand
Not only is it miles that he's eaten
But also eating records that he's beaten
An appetite like all habitual winners
He's had more square meals than you've had hot dinners
His style is resolutely 'Euro-Pro'
Respect reserved for others in the know
Without complaint he'll duly drop the hammer
Whenever his tifosi start to clamour.

A courier is idly standing by
Her filthy frame the apple of her eye
Enamel with a lacquer made of stickers
An arrow aiming at the city slickers
Her bag is like a superhero's cape
With radio holder made of gaffa tape
Controller's voice accompanied by static
Amount of work is seasonally erratic
She never rides without an A-Z
Or LCEF cap upon her head
A journey's more worthwhile if there's a docket
And usually simpler with a single sprocket.

The courier is under observation
The voyeur is a studied imitation
Though he would claim it's more than just an act
Aesthetics preclude being too exact

Some tell-tale signs he's not an all-out clone
Like brand new laptop, tablet, mobile phone
An absence of pollutants in his pores
Acquaintance not been made with saddle sores
He claims his fixie's been a lifelong passion
But rides it like it's going out of fashion
And fakenger is his belittling tag
Because there is no radio on his bag.

The sportiviste has come to cycling late
With labour-saving gadgets on his plate
Like GPS for pinpoint navigation
(If software is the latest iteration)
And though it might prevent him getting lost
It comes at a considerable cost
But spending's not a burden for this MAMIL
Financial backbone stronger than a camel
His carbon frame is monocoque not bonded
He's unaware of anything Lemond did
Reducing heritage to retro clothing
A 39 tooth causes fear and loathing.

A randonneur provides a stark contrast
For him there is no first, there is no last
A bicycle of consummate utility
Not weighted down with gram-saving futility
Protection from the elements all round
A beard up top and mudguards near the ground
Steel tubes and 25s to give respite
From endless miles throughout the day and night
Remaining focussed on the next control
His card is stamped and then it's time to roll
The hours are long, and yet it's not a chore
To boldly go where no man's gone before.

The souplesse of the trackie is renowned
Co-ordinated twitch fibres abound
Acceleration deadly like a cheetah's
Endurance falters at a thousand metres
His loss of motivation is acute
Beyond the standing start of the pursuit
He's not the type to sit within a bunch
The scratch race interferes with plans for lunch
Relentless weights and rollers through the winter
To cultivate the physique of a sprinter
A sojourn on the road from time to time
Invisible until the village sign.

Although he lacks the spark to be explosive
The tester marches on like a corrosive
Imprisoned by the maths of time and distance
Ignoring pain but suffering with persistence
The deepest section front that is permitted
An aero seatpost, disc, and tri-bars fitted
Enhancing FTP is a no-brainer
And so is time spent on the turbo trainer
For some his dimpled skinsuit reeks of frippery
How could this character get any more slippery
If needed he'll resort to the uncouth
And PLF to win the race of truth.

The great rouleur is oozing big ring attitude
From those who wheel-suck she expects no gratitude
Her workmanlike approach is not unique
But steadfast like a super domestique
She's always at the sharp end of an echelon
And won't ignore a call to put the pressure on
No shirking if it's windy, cold, or raining
The weather forecast's always good for training

To blow apart the bunch is de rigeur
The commissaires decree a force majeure
Just sadomasochism through and through
It's going to hurt her more than it hurts you.

A dancer when he stands upon the pedals
The mountain looms, the grimpeur duly treadles
Up every gradient he weaves his way
While others feel their knees start to decay
In gravity he has a confidante
She tells him that he's wrong to think he can't
The vicious slope is mostly in the mind
So turn the screw and leave the rest behind
Eccentric on account of inclination
His power-to-weight a magical equation
The only heaviness a weathered frown
Lamentably what goes up must come down.

All introductions dealt with for the bunch
Let's focus on the journey towards lunch
Though EC1's all very well and good
Some saddle time is better understood
The café owner held the door ajar
Announcing an impromptu grand départ
A ceremony of a modest scale
To mark the true beginning of this tale
So with our jersey pockets hanging low
From carbohydrates we'd exchanged for dough
We moved with purpose back onto the street
Our last step mating pedal with the cleat.

The Roadie's Tale

The roadie leads the group this opening stage
Imploring minds and bodies to engage
Proceeds between the West End and the City
The Elephant and all that nitty-gritty
He'll stay up front across the conurbation
Till Croydon looms in composite formation
The parcours via which he will arrive:
A3 > A23 > A235.

"The tale of my career-defining race
Is something far beyond the commonplace
An hour of speed and general delirium
The kind you'll only find in a criterium
We line up wheel to wheel and rubbing bars
The veterans still as hopeful as espoirs
I feel my legs replete with good sensations
It's not a day for spicy embrocations
Before the signal to commence hostilities
I weigh up rivals and the possibilities:
To force the pace, accelerate, attack
Then feign exhaustion sitting at the back?
Avoid the front aside from the odd stint
And keep my powder dry until the sprint?
To hell with it, I'll cause a big furore
And break away majestically to glory.

I deftly clip my second foot and go
Prepared to make the first decisive blow
The microcosmic race to the first bend
The start can be a portent of the end
Beyond the turn I usher riders through
My elbow flicks and they know what to do
Automatons who readily comply
Their work ethic in bountiful supply
I stir the air to signal a rotation
Perpetual motion of my instigation
They take their turns, but I am faking mine
Soft-pedalling, finessing, serpentine
A lap complete and things begin to settle
It won't be long before I test their mettle
The calm precedes the rider who's the storm
The stage is set and so I must perform.

With stealth at first I start to pull away
A muted fanfare, scrupulous display
Remaining seated, upper body quiet
Not hastening the peloton to riot
But once a corner gives me camouflage
I go full gas while thinking "bon courage!"
Devour the rolling section sur la plaque
And quickly get some distance from the pack
My full commitment is imperative
Take any risk that bucks the will to live
Not brake or flinch or tense or lose my nerve
Or bottle as I pedal through a curve
It's fight and flight combined to great effect
Capitulation something I reject
Continue with my underground incision
And dig a narrow a tunnel for my vision.

Establishing an incremental gap
With each prolonged excruciating lap
Ignoring data I don't need to know
I'll pay attention when it's five to go
Along the way I pick up every prime
Accruing cash and boosting self-esteem
I start to wonder if I'll lap the field
But that is where my hubris is revealed
No sooner have I had my grand delusion
Than suddenly I sense a rude intrusion
Cacophony of spokes and heavy breathing
The realization briefly has me seething
How could I let this interloper bridge?
Now stuck to my back wheel like mucilage
The minute five laps go up on the board
This vulture's staked his claim on my reward.

With negative psychology arrested
I promise to myself I won't be bested
The first thing on my newly formed agenda
To make it crystal clear I don't surrender
A vicious turn of speed down the back straight
But he responds before it is too late
Still undeterred I dish out further pain
He latches on magnetically again
Despite the poker face, I know he's shaken
I'm too experienced to be mistaken
The evidence is always there to find
Attrition of the body and the mind
It doesn't suit the circumspect tactician
To underestimate the opposition
And right on cue comes his attacking move
He bridged the gap but still has more to prove.

His ultimate manoeuvre's pretty drastic
He comes so close to snapping the elastic
The fortitude required to reel him in
Is little more than my desire to win
I'm on his wheel with just one lap remaining
And sucking it, there's no point him complaining
I take a final cautionary look behind
The bunch is out of sight and out of mind
The knowledge that I'm finally out the woods
Comes when I see his hands still on the hoods
They may as well be resting on the tops
As I come round him heaving on the drops
My victory salute is well rehearsed
My entry fee is amply reimbursed
I celebrate with members of my club
By spending all my winnings in the pub."

The Courier's Tale

The London Sunday morning hurly-burly
Diminishes before the gates of Purley
Concluding vestiges of urban sprawl
Another metaphoric city wall
And just before the leap into the sticks
The courier performs on armoured slicks
She cannot wait till Surrey's hills and valleys
To be an alley cat you need some alleys.

"The battered pair of Sidis on my feet
A pestle to the mortar of the street
Reduced to pounding pavements in frustration
When tyres and banks have problems with inflation
For dwelling at the sharp end of economy
Gives rise to times of undesired autonomy
Reserving spots on steps and walls and benches
No wear and tear created for the wrenches
An empty bag's not heavy but my heart is
I think I'm not the same as how Descartes is
To be, for me, exists outside of thought
While moving packages from port to port
But now my lunch is eaten by mid-morning
And boredom overshadows like an awning
The sky is looking ominously grey
I hope I won't be killing time all day.

Another messenger (or is it courier?
I'm cursed with being a born semantic worrier)
Rolls up in my secluded patch of greenery
We both take in some cake in lieu of scenery
He got it as a freebie from a vendor
All nuts and chocolate in organic splendour
It complements the coffee in my flask
The sun comes out, we sit awhile and bask
Nostalgia typifies our conversation
The golden age of total concentration
A seamless dot-to-dot around the circuit
The randomness a plus, if you could work it
So many things about the job to learn
A single postcode job, wait and return
Occasionally getting on a train
The money, friends, and fun we stood to gain.

An urgent crackle interrupts our reverie
Perhaps a sign the market's in recovery
I'm told to do a job "quick as you can"
As if by now I didn't know the plan
The exenger who thinks that he controls us
His operandi better than his modus
He does the desk job that he once eschewed
At times his envy makes him rather rude
I head towards the City's concrete fingers
Where half the workforce aimlessly malingers
They drift into my path without a care
All disapproving looks or vacant stare
But when they show up at their corporate castle
And see upon their desk an urgent parcel
They ought to be aware of gift and giver
Whenever London needs me, I deliver."

XII
I
II
III
IV
V
VI
VII
VIII
IX
X
XI

The Sportiviste's Tale

The nomansland beyond the buzzing hive
Horizon formed by the M25
Is where the sportiviste goes to the front
Apparently prepared to bear the brunt
On witnessing his over-zealous move
The others wonder what he's trying to prove
He wants to get his story put to bed
Before the Col de Whyteleafe rears its head.

"You have to pay a premium to be
A rider of a certain pedigree
Componentry that's at the cutting edge and
Apparel that presents you as a legend
Invest in an aesthetic which will last
Contemporary but rooted in the past
And when you stop to order cappuccino
Insist that the barista wears merino
Nutrition must be cycling-specific
All training regimens are scientific
Analysis of power by a coach
Holistic and meticulous approach
The comfort from my bike-fit consultation
Pays dividends commuting from the station
I emulate the riders of the Tour
My colleagues in the City are in awe.

Preparing for La Marmotte and L'Étape
Concurrent physical and fiscal trap
Both credit card and heart rate hit their max
Fatigue and debt launch crippling attacks
Maintaining top tier groupsets is expensive
When damage from a stack ends up extensive
The aches and pains take longer to evaporate
Now youth is something I no longer celebrate
But it will all be worth it in the end
If only for the option to descend
A sweeping mountain road for half an hour
The thrill of speed without the need for power
Encouragement from continental folk
The latent inner strength it will evoke
Triumphant photographs to share online
It will be mine, oh yes, it will be mine.

With winter written off due to the weather
As collarbones and ice don't go together
Aerobic base is not what I'd projected
But springtime sees my body resurrected
Some steady miles continue as insurance
If nothing else it should improve endurance
Intensity, however, is still lacking
There's suddenly no time for any slacking
I pick a training loop that will provide
The challenges I need during a ride
A thoroughly obscene amount of climbing
Analysis of altitude and timing
Descents that cause my fingers to go numb
And corners where your fears are overcome
I'll be prepared and ready to embark
All thanks to epic laps of Richmond Park."

The Trackie's Tale

Declining the ability to coast
Is not a choice that would appeal to most
But in this group progressing to the sea
I've made that choice, as have another three
For one of them it's reflex and instinctive
Not knee-jerk though, their smoothness is distinctive
The trackie pedals like a Magimix®
Especially spinning down a 1-in-6.

"There isn't room for any kind of fear in
The velodrome when riding in the keirin
Each rider stands before the rising sun
A colour of the rainbow every one
Their form and horoscopes have been appraised
All bets are placed, the starting pistol raised
And gambling here's accomplished with impunity
As funds will go to helping the community
Formality's a given in Japan
The NJS dictates the artisan
From A-class up to S-class you proceed
Respect the lines to maximise your speed
Nine riders raise their cadence with the gong
Success is for the canny and the strong
A sense of order permeates the sport
But where I race there's chaos to report.

The English climate's famously unsettled
Components inexpediently fettled
There is no cure for badly fitted tubs
Or suicidal tendencies with hubs
And novices abound in unknown territory
Some have the legs but fail at the respiratory
Their dangerous machines cobbled together
Like Belgian pavé in inclement weather
The dernys hibernate for months on end
Wake up in time to see the long weekend
Protecting experts from the vernal wind
A moving wall on which their hopes are pinned
But then it's umpteen also-rans like me
Week in, week out, or intermittently
Relearn our craft afresh with each new year
All summer gains annulled by winter beer.

Most often there's no motor for our pacer
We wind it up behind another racer
A chance for them to keep their muscles loose
Between their bouts of ritual self-abuse
Aware that there's a scarcity of judges
Some people go before the pacer budges
Resulting in a messy one-lap dash
A wave of senkos heading for a crash
But luckily my legspeed gets me clear
Avoiding falling bodies to the rear
I learnt to pedal quickly as a boy
A muscle memory that I still enjoy
Just three of us surviving at the finish
Conjoined with no intention to diminish
At times like these there's just one way to cope
You hold your line and then you lunge and hope."

THE
RISINGSUN

The Rouleur's Tale

The rolling road from Bletchingley is fast
To ride it with a tailwind is a blast
It's here the rouleur takes her rightful place
She drives the group at a remorseless pace
To chaperone the weary is her calling
We're hypnotised, her power is enthralling
It seems as if she's grown bored of Surrey
And wants to get to Sussex in a hurry.

"We met in March along a country lane
He practically unshipped me like a chain
Though normally a rider who's undroppable
The force with which he moved me was unstoppable
On flat terrain I almost came to rest
Impeded but concurrently impressed
Our first entanglement was just the start
He courted me until he won my heart
Our intimacy deepened with each ride
At times I laughed, at times I nearly cried
He got up in my face from time to time
But pedalling in tandem was sublime
Occasionally his absence was conspicuous
I'd grown to recognise him as ubiquitous
When I was slow he was my caveat
Contriving draggy climbs when things were flat.

Avoiding our relationship's demise
Involved a fair amount of compromise
Whenever I had nothing left to give
By changing tack he'd be a sedative
Through him my deadspots were eliminated
Against him I no longer fulminated
With humour I absorbed his playful blows
Swept him aside on big gear ratios
My growing fortitude brought admiration
Engendered not a hint of indignation
He knew that those who chose to suck my wheel
Would suffer greatly as part of the deal
A gradual dawning that it might be worse
To hide from him and use me to traverse
The countryside on which he liked to roam
I sensed that many wished they'd stayed at home.

Our partnership is based upon equality
But don't presume it's lacking in frivolity
Attrition rubs up many the wrong way
For us, however, it's a form of play
We partly represent laws of attraction
Though too equal and opposite reaction
Inseparable, completely symbiotic
To come between us might be deemed psychotic
We ride as if a single organism
And even after death there'll be no schism
Behaving as described by Sergeant Pluck
The two of us will be forever stuck
It is the way of all the world's flahutes
To join the weather and be in cahoots
And so this metaphor has underpinned
The tale of how I learnt to love the wind."

The Fakenger's Tale

To classify a climb is quite subjective
Both weight and fitness alter your perspective
Puncheurs will blink and miss a hill like Turners
But it's a distant stare for fixie learners
Today is no exception to the rule
The fakenger has geared up like a fool
No brakes attached, his tyres are hard and skiddy
A fourteen in the back, up front a fiddy.

"So what's the toughest and the quietest chain?
And which tyres skid, but grip well in the rain?
How narrow should I cut my risers down?
Are bullhorns best for when you ride in town?
Is 49/13 good for commuting?
Are online auctions ever worth disputing?
Can I remove the brake track from these rims?
Which brand of beercan is the best for shims?
Is there a saddle that'll work with jeans?
Does anybody know what hipster means?
And where's the most authentic place to ride?
Who thinks my sitbones are unusually wide?
What pressure should I run to make me faster?
For white tyres: ivory, cream, or alabaster?
How can I Pantone match this shade of blue?
I've bought a fixie, who knows what to do?

What difference will one tooth make on a sprocket?
Who else rides with their D-lock in their pocket?
Will I fall off the first time I try clipless?
Should I keep pista drops untaped and gripless?
Is riding brakeless actually much safer?
Whose clearances are thinner than a wafer?
Why won't my lefthand pedal come unscrewed?
Who else is sick of couriers' attitude?
How many patches for an ambi-skidder?
Which track hubs for the road would you consider?
Has anybody tried ceramic bearings?
Will odours vanish with repeated airings?
Are cranksets made of alloy way too flexy?
Do peds and nodders cause you apoplexy?
Who's feeling pangs of existential sorrow?
Has someone got a light that I can borrow?

Will mudguards spoil the clean lines of my frame?
Are 531 and 653 the same?
Which lacing pattern with these high-flange hubs?
Who knows the good routes used by local clubs?
How can I stop this aching in my knees?
Are chainrings from this company made of cheese?
What stuff is always carried in your bag?
Do woolen jersey pockets always sag?
Can someone recommend a set of rollers?
Should fakengers have radios and controllers?
So which is quicker: singlespeed or gears?
Do headphones change the way a rider hears?
It's helmet time, who wants a mass debate?
How can you stop at reds and not be late?
Is fixiedom a chapel or a church?
Are newbies ever going to use the search?"

The Randonneur's Tale

From Turners Hill to Ardingly and on
All memories of waking up are gone
The straightish tree-lined road becomes a blur
And at the front we find the randonneur
This 100k from London to the shingle
Will only cause his legs a mild tingle
The others know that when they board the train
He'll turn around and do the same again.

"There is a certain place I like to ride
To get there I spend many hours outside
Beyond the pressing walls of time and space
Without the agitation of a race
It isn't in a solitary location
But can exist in total isolation
Alone or in a swollen peloton
Perception alters at the Rubicon
The stamps on brevet cards prove that I've been
Along the secret roads which run between
Subconscious signposts pointing one direction
Past any thoughts of lasting imperfection
My badges and my patches tell a tale
Of all the dizzy heights I've had to scale
The dreich and sunken valleys that I've crossed
Occasions when I feared all hope was lost.

It's often when I enter the crepuscular
With lights that aren't extravagantly muscular
I see a golden ratio appear
And start to shift without a change of gear
Diverse abstract realities are linked
All boundaries reframed as indistinct
A dark and graduated composition
The sky distills the blues from my cognition
Hypnosis happens in the wee small hours
Sleep deprivation almost overpowers
My shoulders droop, my eyelids feeling heavy
Subconscious streams of thought burst through the levee
Perhaps I'll slumber at the village hall
Lay on the floor and curl up in a ball
But once I've had a coffee and some cake
It feels like sleeping would be a mistake.

Another stamp and back out on the road
Not long before my senses all implode
Intense hallucinations congregate
I start to question what will be my fate
Rear LEDs spell cryptic words of warning
Implying legions of the damned are spawning
I'm hounded from the roadside by dissenters
A multitude of Stygian tormentors
Eventually, however, they dissolve
An optimistic sunrise sparks resolve
To come this far and quit would be demented
My pride would be irrevocably dented
The audax is a study of persistence
An exercise in how to go the distance
Despite the tribulations and the trials
There's boundless joy in racking up the miles.

The Tester's Tale

With mouths like chainrings full of gritted teeth
The group is strung out after Haywards Heath
A tester on the front and level ground
Has seen a rise in pace that's quite profound
Reminded that he has a tale to tell
He eases up for slower personnel
They catch their breath, recover from the shock
Then hear about the race against the clock.

"Pushed into action by the burly holder
And time-keeper who's just a little older
Atrocious weather seeming inhumane
I pass another marshall in the rain
With elbows tucked together near the stem
A mumbled mantra, pacing stratagem
To lift my head, my neck a constant crane
I pass another marshall in the rain
It takes a while for everything to settle
Become the bike, flesh, composite, and metal
Ride through the first few miles of teething pain
I pass another marshall in the rain
The movement of my joints begins to mesh
It feels as though I start the race afresh
My breathing is a rhythmical refrain
I pass another marshall in the rain.

Has it been worth the training protocol
The turbo binge instead of alcohol
So hard to overreach not overtrain
I pass another marshall in the rain
A float day on a fast course would be nice
Just once within my lifetime would suffice
Submission of the air you can't explain
I pass another marshall in the rain
Inside my head are sequences of numbers
Dividing the existence which encumbers
Dissociation helps to take the strain
I pass another marshall in the rain
Alertness re-engages for the turn
As roundabouts and slip roads cause concern
And then there's my momentum to regain
I pass another marshall in the rain.

Historically we've kept things surreptitious
Fraternity of roadies are suspcious
They view our discipline with some disdain
I pass another marshall in the rain
Intense exertion at the crack of dawn
The suffering is a curve on which I learn
Performance is enhanced most by the brain
I pass another marshall in the rain
Dual-carriageway spools past like celluloid
The threshold crossed, I'm slicing through the void
A chequered flag the goal I must attain
I pass another marshall in the rain
When all is said and done I travel home
The clock ticks on, eternal metronome
It's marginal the edge we seek to gain
I pass another marshall in the rain."

The Grimpeur's Tale

Along this coastal region runs a spine
A wall of green before the finish line
To reach the end involves a test of will
The grimpeur leads the charge when it's uphill
He moves ahead with purpose at the bottom
Then shrinks into the distance till forgotten
But waiting at the top is where he'll be
His breathing shallow, staring at the sea.

"Of all the hills and mountains that I've ridden
There's one that has a peak remaining hidden
The most demanding of them all by far
Carved into human memory like a scar
Throughout its course the gradient mutates
A sense of weighing down never abates
You jettison your baggage in despair
And suckle at the teat of thinning air
The early ramps are shockingly severe
Disorientating to the inner ear
Extreme sensations past your comfort zone
You're disconnected, vulnerable, alone
To some extent the learning curve relents
But not for long on treacherous ascents
There's always something just around the bend
That hastens all complacency to end.

Fragility can be a kind of strength
The cracks acquired across your breadth and length
Are things you take great pains to guard from harm
And overcoming doubt works like a charm
If what's ahead's perceived as insurmountable
You mentally divide it so it's countable
The whole's no greater than some of its parts
When one's been done that's where completion starts
Sometimes it feels as though you're barely moving
Or things will likely never start improving
A new approach is often all that's needed
For impetus renewed and unimpeded
Experience should bless you with sagacity
Inform you to engage your full capacity
Remaining seated just won't cut the mustard
You need to stand to get things done and dusted.

The further up you go, the more you see
It's all spread out below, a tapestry
Exhibiting the landscape you've traversed
The ups and downs with plateaus interspersed
But satisfying though the view may be
Admiring it can't last indefinitely
When thoughts of finishing preoccupy
Your focus once again turns to the sky
The process is a magical transition
A higher plane – through pain – the acquisition
It takes you via the gamut of the bestial
Until you find the peaceful and celestial
When gravity is tamed you feel enlightened
An out of body state, no longer frightened
And on the day you reach the very top
You'll hear a voice that says it's time to stop."

Epilogue

The runway into town negotiated
Along the promenade we're congregated
We grab the food for which we've travelled far
Then park our bikes outside The Evening Star
With drinks in hand we contemplate the ride
Collectively we glow from the inside
But words alone can't capture how it feels
The thrill of time spent moving on two wheels
Dear reader, it is sometimes worth recalling
The moment when you lost your fear of falling
When Mum or Dad let go without you knowing
Internal brakes released, no sign of slowing
This sense of liberation never dwindles
It's something that the bicycle rekindles
To guarantee a healthy constitution
You turn the cranks and start a revolution.

www.ingramcontent.com/pod-product-compliance
Ingram Content Group UK Ltd.
Pitfield, Milton Keynes, MK11 3LW, UK
UKHW041837200726
13854UKWH00003BA/1175

9 781291 127829